D0493120

THE
**PAUL HAMLYN
LIBRARY**

DONATED BY
THE PAUL HAMLYN
FOUNDATION
TO THE
BRITISH MUSEUM

WITHDRAWN

opened December 2000

STORY OF THE NILE

ILLUSTRATED BY STEVE NOON

WRITTEN BY DR ANNE MILLARD

DORLING KINDERSLEY

London • New York • Munich • Melbourne • Delhi

CONTENTS

932
WITHDRAWN
THE BRITISH MUSEUM
THE PAUL HAMLYN LIBRARY

DK

A Dorling Kindersley Book

Editors Zahavit Shalev and Linda Esposito
Designer Diane Thistlethwaite
Production Linda Dare
Jacket design Christopher Branfield

First published in Great Britain in 2003
by Dorling Kindersley Limited
80 Strand, London WC2R 0RL

A Penguin Company

2 4 6 8 10 9 7 5 3 1

Copyright © 2003 Dorling Kindersley Limited

All rights reserved. No part of this publication may be
reproduced, stored in a retrieval system, or transmitted in any
form or by any means, electronic, mechanical, photocopying,
recording, or otherwise, without the prior written permission
of the copyright owner.

A CIP catalogue record for this book
is available from the British Library.

ISBN 0-7513-6827-X

Colour reproduction by Dot Gradations, UK.
Printed and bound in Singapore by Tien Wah Press

THE STORY OF THE NILE

Take a journey along some 7,000 kilometres (4,350 miles) from the source of the Nile to the Mediterranean Sea. At its source, the river is called the White Nile. We follow its course across plains full of game, through rocky gorges and tropical forests, and into an impenetrable swamp. At the site of the modern city of Khartoum it merges with another river, the Blue Nile. Then, nature plays a trick. For the last 1,800 km (1,120 miles) of its journey the Nile flows through a desert!

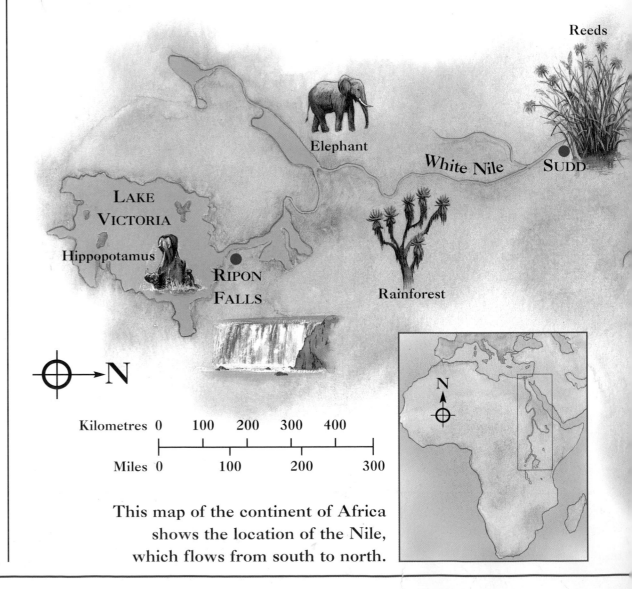

Reeds

Elephant

White Nile

SUDD

LAKE VICTORIA

Hippopotamus

RIPON FALLS

Rainforest

N

Kilometres 0   100   200   300   400

Miles 0   100   200   300

N

This map of the continent of Africa
shows the location of the Nile,
which flows from south to north.

Finally the river divides into several channels, flowing through the rich farm land of the Delta into the Mediterranean Sea. However, each year, when the melting snow and the spring rains in the mountains of Ethiopia surge down the Blue Nile and into the Nile proper, the river north of Khartoum floods. These life-giving waters gave birth to one of the world's oldest civilizations and continue to make life possible for the modern nations living in the region today.

Our guide on this journey is a magic pelican, flying through time as well as space. Through him we will see how the Nile has influenced all aspects of the life of its people, and witness some of the epic events that took place during its long history. We'll see the great kingdoms that flourished along its banks, and the ordinary people who have relied on the mighty Nile for their survival.

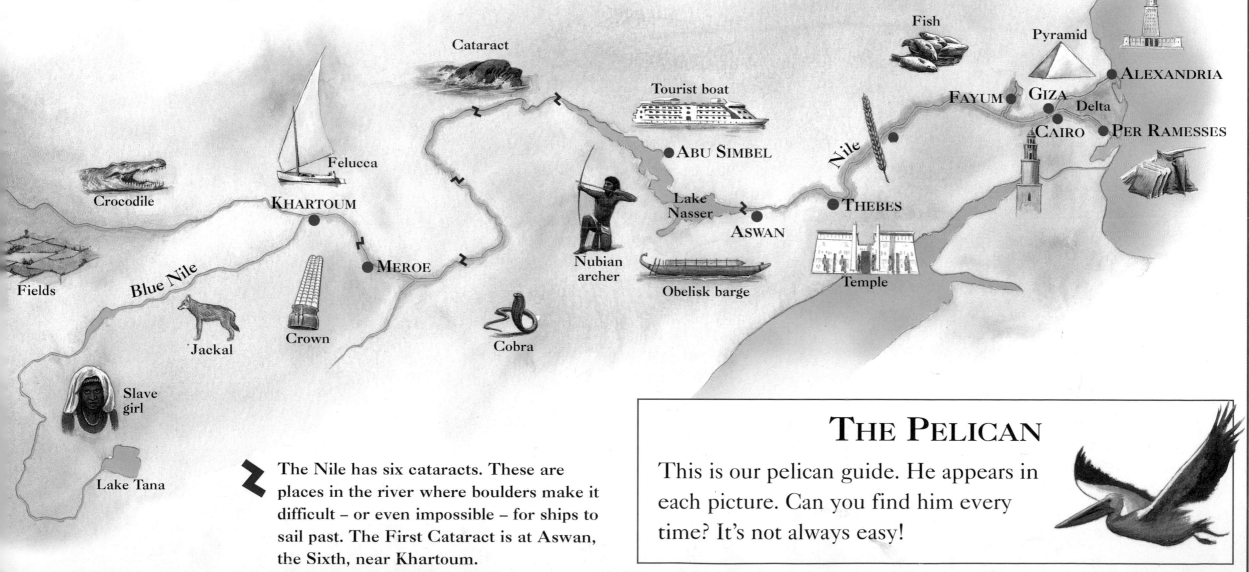

Fish

Pyramid

Cataract

Tourist boat

ALEXANDRIA

FAYUM

GIZA

Delta

Nile

ABU SIMBEL

CAIRO

PER RAMESSES

Felucca

KHARTOUM

Lake Nasser

THEBES

Crocodile

ASWAN

Nubian archer

MEROE

Obelisk barge

Temple

Jackal

Crown

Cobra

Blue Nile

Fields

Slave girl

Lake Tana

The Nile has six cataracts. These are places in the river where boulders make it difficult – or even impossible – for ships to sail past. The First Cataract is at Aswan, the Sixth, near Khartoum.

THE PELICAN

This is our pelican guide. He appears in each picture. Can you find him every time? It's not always easy!

THE SOURCE OF THE NILE
Ripon Falls, Lake Victoria, 28th July 1862 AD

Englishman John Speke stands by Lake Victoria and watches its waters spill into the Nile. Many explorers have set out to discover the source of the River Nile but none have succeeded until now. He names the 142 m (66 ft) wide waterfall the Ripon Falls.

Lionesses

Thompson's gazelles

Goliath heron

Wildebeest

Zebra

Hartebeest

Ripon Falls

Rainbow

Hippopotamuses

Fish eagle

Find the fishermen trying to escape from some angry hippopotamuses.

Where do the local villagers wash their clothes?

4

The head guide, Sidi Bombay, is in charge of the porters. He is paid 60 dollars a year.

A palisade around their village protects the people and their cattle from wild animals.

Storks

Village

Thatched-houses

Lake Victoria

Collecting firewood

Cattle

Washing clothes

Fisherman

Fish

Building shelter

Collecting water

Harpooning fish

John Speke's tent

John Speke

Porters

Crocodiles

Sidi Bombay

Preparing food

Find the Goliath heron. It is the largest heron in the world.

Two hungry lionesses are on the lookout for food. Can you see them?

The local people make a living by farming, as well as fishing.

The lake has a good supply of fish, which are carried over the falls. This makes a fisherman's job easy!

How many crocodiles can you see?

The slaves that the Romans have brought along come from all over the Roman Empire.

THE WORLD'S BIGGEST SWAMP
The Sudd, c. 62 AD

The Nile flows north through a changing scenery of lush tropical forest and grassy plains. Then it enters a vast swamp called the Sudd, which is more than 650 km (400 miles) long. There are only three channels through the Sudd, and all are infested with snakes, crocodiles, and insects. Emperor Nero has sent a scouting party to look for new lands to conquer south of Egypt, but the Sudd is proving too much even for these tough Roman soldiers.

Local fisherman

Drying fish

Dragonfly

Insects

Boatmen

Doctor

Slaves

Stores

Centurions

Crested crane

Soldiers

6

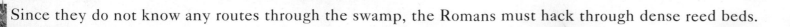

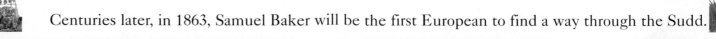

Flamingos

Spoonbill

Swallows

Shoebill

Cobra

Shields

Slave from Britain

Slave

Crocodile

The swamp is a breeding ground for malaria-carrying mosquitoes. Who is feeling ill?

Which soldier is afraid of snakes?

7

SLAVE CITY

Khartoum, c. 1840 AD

The Blue Nile, which begins in Ethiopia, flows into the White Nile at Khartoum. When the Egyptians conquered northern Sudan in 1821, they made this village their headquarters. Khartoum is now a rich trading city. People come from far and wide to buy its main commodities – slaves and elephant tusks for the ivory trade.

Find the pelican. Who is after him?

European and American traders come to Khartoum to buy ivory for luxury goods.

Feluccas

Mudbrick house

Wealthy Egyptian

Unloading ivory

European explorers

Basket maker

European artist

Haggling

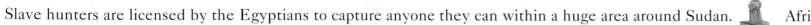

Minaret

East bank

Blue Nile

European traders

White Nile

Ethiopian slave girls

Slave dealer

Beautiful girls have been torn from their families in Ethiopia to be sold in Khartoum.

Spot the local "takeaway".

Coffee shop

Hookah pipe

Bidding for slaves

Guard

Slaves

Slave

Master

Egyptian soldiers

KINGDOM OF GOLD
The Royal City of Meroe, c. 50 AD

Meroe lies between the Third and Sixth Nile Cataracts. It grew out of the land called Kush by the Egyptians, who once ruled much of it and whose influence can still be felt. Meroe is immensely wealthy. One writer tells us that even the prisoners have gold chains! This audience in the palace courtyard is being held to celebrate a military victory.

Egyptian-style buildings

Giraffe

African traders

Indian traders

Incense burner

Iron sword and spear

Spices

Nubian prisoners

King's warrior

Courtiers

High priest

Priestess

Can you spot the bust of the Roman Emperor? Some uninvited spectators are getting a terrific view. Can you spot them?

Meroe's High Priest has just led a service in the temple to give thanks for victory against Nubian raiders. Nubian prisoners kneel before the king and beg for mercy.

Meroe attracts traders from many lands because of its gold, iron, cotton, and exotic animals.

Elephants are tamed and used in war, as well as in royal processions.

In Meroe, large ladies are much admired. The Queen Mother is very powerful. Can you spot her giving the king advice?

Nile

Egyptian-style crowns

King

Queen Mother

Roman Senator

Roman soldiers

Queen

Princess

Courtiers

Ethiopian traders

Royal nurse

Princess

Princes

Precious spices

King's pet leopard

Gold and silver

Fan bearer

Rome is interested in Meroe's wealth. A visiting senator is presenting some horses to the king as a gift.

The king shows off his wealth and power to foreign visitors.

11

BORDER FORT
Nubia, c. 1850 BC

The Nile has been used to carry soldiers and supplies for thousands of years. Since conquering Nubia, the Egyptians have built huge forts to protect their new frontier. Nubia is rich in gold, copper, and precious stones so the forts are also important trading centres. A new governor is arriving to take over at this fort.

Can you spot who almost stood on a snake?

New soldiers are arriving by boat to begin a tour of duty at the fort.

Vultures

Nubian village

Soldiers' barges

Nile

Grain barge

Governor's furniture

Local traders

Governor's hunting dogs

Governor and wife

Guard of honour

Donkeys

Guard

Officer

Army patrol

12

The fort can be approached either by river or land. A heavily-defended land gate reduces the risk of an attack.

This caravan is taking goods north to Egypt.

Government scribes keep a record of all trade to and from the fort.

How many guards can you count on the fort walls?

Fort cattle

Soldiers' families

Donkey caravan

Scribes

Guard dog

Kushite spies

Lizard

Jerboa

13

Many archers in the Egyptian army come from Nubia, which the Egyptians call "Land of the Bow".

These spies come from the warlike Kingdom of Kush, south of Nubia.

TOURISTS AT THE TEMPLES

Abu Simbel, present day

In 1971 the Egyptian government opened the High Dam. As the waters built up south of it, Nubia drowned under Lake Nasser, the biggest artificial lake in the world. Before the dam opened, a huge rescue operation was mounted to save Nubia's ancient monuments. Some of the great temples, like these at Abu Simbel, were cut up into thousands of blocks and rebuilt on higher ground.

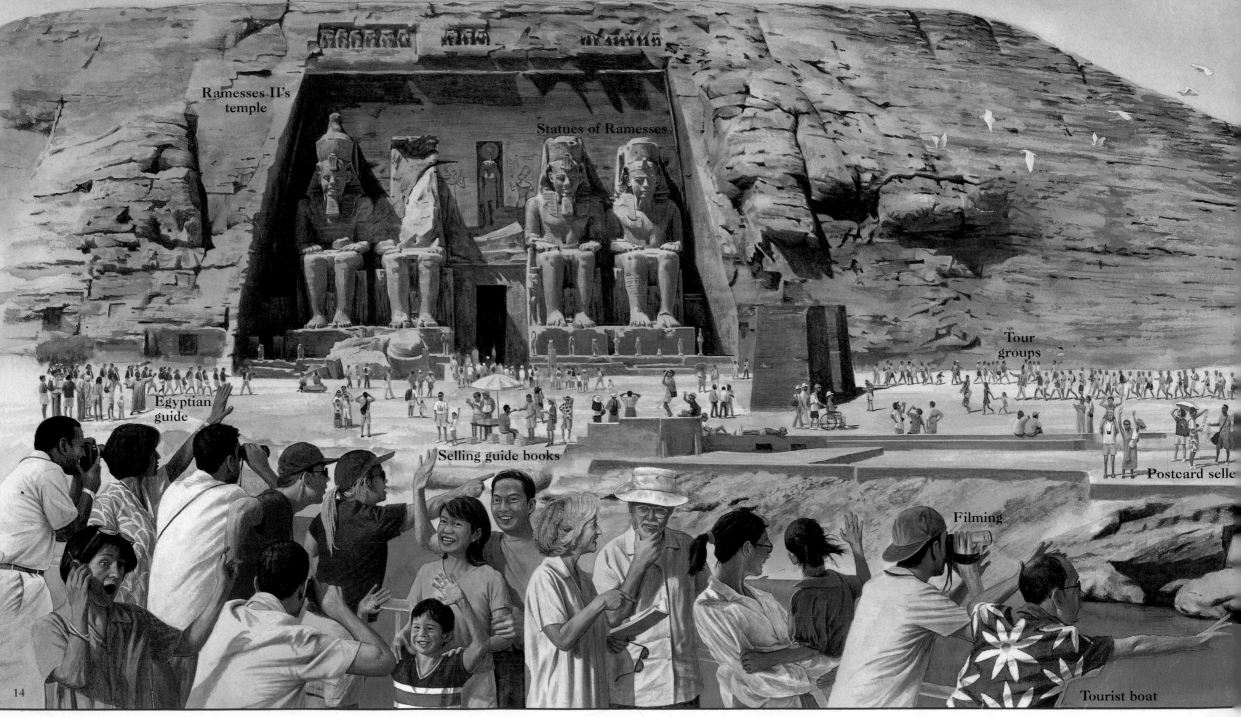

Ramesses II's temple

Statues of Ramesses

Egyptian guide

Selling guide books

Tour groups

Postcard selle[r]

Filming

Tourist boat

14

Can you spot the group of tourists who are all wearing the same hats?

Tourism is very important to Egypt's economy.

As in ancient times, twice a year the rising sun lights up the gods' statues in the temple's inner sanctuary.   Planes, boats, and coaches bring in hundreds of tourists daily.

Ramesses built a temple for his favourite wife, Nefertari. Ramesses fathered almost two hundred children. Some are represented by statues outside the temple.

Nefertari's temple

The dam exists to make sure Egypt has a regular water supply.

Ramesses built the most monuments of any pharaoh.

Selling sun hats

Temple guardian with key

Selling cold drinks

Nile (Lake Nasser)

Police boat

The temples were carved out of the mountain and took four years to move. Mass tourism began in 1869 when Thomas Cook began organizing trips to Egypt.

Rollers are used to drag heavy objects. Pouring water over them helps the statue glide smoothly.

A herd of cattle is being led to safety through the river.

EGYPT'S HIGHWAY

Aswan, c. 1500 BC

The quickest and easiest way to move people and heavy goods is on the river. The best time to shift stone from quarries to building projects is between July and October, when the Nile comes closest to the quarries while flooding all the flat farming land between the desert cliffs. Here, a giant barge carries obelisks from the Aswan granite quarries north to the Karnak temple in Thebes.

Can you find the man who has fallen overboard?

Rich people can afford to be carried, but everyone else walks.

Temple of Khnum

Elephantine Island

Obelisk

Royal messenger's boat

Senmut's barge

Boat wrecks

Cattle barge

Noble lady

Huntsmen

Steward

Scribe

Servant

Wine

Noble in chariot

16

Nubian archers are sailing north to join the Egyptian army.

Senmut is the architect in charge of the obelisk project. He is travelling alongside the obelisk

Former governors of Aswan are buried in tombs in the desert cliffs.

The Temple of Khnum, the god responsible for the annual flooding, is on Elephantine Island.

Nobles' tombs

Boats towing barge

Fishing boats

Nubian archers

Steering oar

Grain barge

Ferry

Housewife

17

Chariots are used for battle and for hunting in the desert.

The rocks and the fast-flowing rapids of the First Cataract at Aswan pose a danger to ships.

THE FEAST OF OPET

Thebes, c. 1180 BC

The Nile is so important in the daily lives of ancient Egyptians that it also features significantly in their religious beliefs. Here in Thebes, a great river procession is bringing the statue of the god Amun from his main temple at Karnak to his second temple to celebrate his life-giving powers. The festival is called Opet. It lasts for eleven days and attracts great crowds.

Ibis

Entrance to temple

Obelisk

Statue of Ramesses II

Flag pole

White walls

Statues of sacred baboons

Fan bearers

Libyan captives

Ramesses III

18

At festivals, some people are overcome by religious excitement. 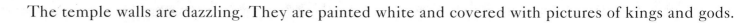 The temple walls are dazzling. They are painted white and covered with pictures of kings and gods.

Cliffs

Funeral procession

Pilgrims' boats

Amun's barge

Priests

Shrine

HighPriest

Priestesses   Petitioner

Musicians

Dancers

Offerings

Guards

Any Egyptian can approach the god's statue and ask for help with a problem. Who is in trouble for drinking too much beer?

Ibises and baboons are sacred to Thoth, the god of wisdom.   When statues of gods have to be moved they are put in shrines on small boats and carried by priests.

EVERY LAST DROP
Middle Egypt, c. 1560 AD

Since Egypt has so little rain, water for crops comes from the Nile. Ancient Egyptians discovered how to save the waters of the flood each year and carry it in canals and ditches round their fields. The Arabs who conquered Egypt use the same system. Like their ancestors, these peasants grow grain, flax, vegetables, and fruit.

Washing clothes

Camel

Felucca

Date palms

Shaduf

Cattle

Can you find the nasty boy bullying his younger brother?

Somebody has to climb the tree to get to the ripe dates.

20

Church

Goats

Muezzin

Flax

Ancient tombs

Christian
ceremony

Pigeon lofts

Wheat

Mosque

Oven

Pilgrims

Funeral
procession

Canal

Carpenters

Potter

Water
wheel

Chickens

21

THE GIFTS OF THE NILE
The Fayum, c. 1890 BC

Water for drinking, bathing, and watering crops comes from the Nile. The river provides a plentiful supply of fish and wild birds to eat, as well as reeds that can be made into anything from boats to paper. To this elderly nobleman and his family, sport and relaxation are other gifts of the Nile.

Palm trees

Building a reed boat

Bundles of reeds

Collecting water

Hippo hunting

Spear fishing

Birds caught in net

Bird catchers

Servant

Nobleman's eldest son

Wife

Pied kingfisher

Daughter

Reed boat

Lotus

Can you spot the children playing with toy boats?

The pelican has had a lucky escape from a net. Can you see him?

22

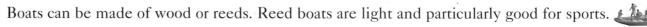

Exotic animals like monkeys are imported from lands further south.

The lotus is a sacred flower. How many can you count?

Pyramid

Papyrus reeds

Fishing

Cutting reeds

Washing clothes

Water joust

Pet monkey

Steersman

Nobleman

Shield

Nurse

Daughter

Nurse

Sailors

Playing flute

Oars

Steering oar

Wife

Servant

Picnic

Plumb line

Wooden boat

Son

23

THE FUNERAL OF KING KHUFU

Giza, c. 2500 BC

This is the funeral of King Khufu. The sun and the river are central to daily life in Egypt so they also shape people's ideas about the afterlife. The Egyptians believe that their king is the son of Re, the sun god, who journeys through the underworld Kingdom of the Dead at night. Khufu's body is being ferried over the Nile to the west bank where the sun sets. It will be laid to rest inside a huge pyramid whose shape reflects the sun's rays.

Pyramid of King Khufu

Pyramids for the three queens

Falcon

Small palace

Mortuary temple

Causeway

Offerings of food and animals

Statue

Royal bodyguard

Funeral boat

Trained mourners

Harbour

Egrets

24

Can you spot the new king and queen?

Egyptians believe the sky god, Horus, can visit earth as a falcon. Can you see one?

The funeral boats are buried near to the pyramid so that King Khufu can sail alongside the sun in the afterlife. Women mourners wail and splash their faces with mud.

Pigeons

Date palms

Valley temple

Priestesses with sistrums and flowers

New king and queen

Coffin placed on model boat

Soldiers

Noblemen and women mourners

Lector Priest reading prayers

High priest

Royal family

Chief Queen

Prince Khafra

Can you see the children who have sneaked in to get a good view? Can you see Khafra sulking because he is not the new king?

A ceremony in the mortuary temple gives the dead king back all his bodily senses. The Chief Queen is the most important wife. Her sons are first in line for the throne.

Saladin is of Kurdish descent but he controls a huge Middle Eastern empire that includes Egypt.

An aqueduct carries water from the Nile up to the Citadel.

Can you see a rich man being carried in a sedan chair?

Muslim women wear veils when they go out out in public.

A Hero Sets Out

Cairo, c. 1190 AD

Here, the great Muslim leader, Salah el Din, or Saladin sets off to fight the Christian armies in the Third Crusade. After the Muslim Arabs had conquered Egypt in 640 AD, they built Cairo at the place where the Nile divides into several channels, and made it their capital. A great fortress – the Citadel – built on a rocky outcrop protects the city.

Camel caravan

Dancing girls

Barber

Goats

Nubian maid

Snake charmer

Soldiers

Saladin

26

Muslim scholarship and lifestyle are superior to those of Europe. Cairo has schools, universities, mosques and public baths.

Rich men go hunting with hawks.

Wooden grilles on windows give the women indoors privacy. 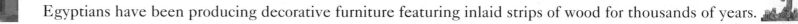 Egyptians have been producing decorative furniture featuring inlaid strips of wood for thousands of years.

Cairo is built from blocks that belonged to the pyramids in Giza.

Can you see who is throwing a flower to Saladin?

Citadel

Mosque

Minaret

Bath house

Aqueduct

Wooden balcony

Furniture

Shoes

Textiles

Rugs

Copper

Spices

Scribe

Beggar

Bedouin

Water seller

27

The Crusades are being fought by Muslims and Christians for control of the Holy Land.  Arab traders do business as far away as central Asia and China.

Medjay are the local police force. Many policemen are Nubians but most officers are Egyptians.

Libyans and Sherden are disliked because they frequently invade Egypt.

INTERNATIONAL RELATIONS
Per Ramesses, c. 1260 BC

Diplomats and traders always use the Nile when they come to do business in Egypt. This is the new city of Per Ramesses built by King Ramesses II on an eastern branch of the Nile. Its location allows the King to keep an eye on his great rivals, the Hittites, who want to take over Egypt's eastern empire.

Can you see how a woman is carrying her baby?

Egyptians do not mind foreigners worshipping their own gods.

Egyptian warship

Nubian ship

Imported timber

Ambassador from Mycenae

Beer shop

Oil

Grain

Canaanite traders from Byblos

Medjay

Scribe

Local ship

Ivory

Foreman

28

Dogs are common in Egypt. They are used for hunting and guarding, and people also keep them as pets.

Some of the Habiru slaves may actually be Hebrews.

Bedouins live in desert regions, moving around with their flocks between watering holes. 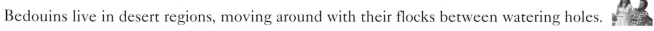 Egyptian officials are welcoming the new ambassador from Mycenae and his wife.

Pylon gate under construction

Habiru slaves

Mudbrick city wall

Decorated gateway

Scribes are important because not everyone can read and write.

Canaanite shrine

Dancer and musician

Ostrich feathers

Imported horses

Wine

Hittite spies

Watermelons

Can you see Hittite spies gathering information?

Libyans

Hittite woman with bodyguard

Thief

Bedouin from Sinai

Nubians

29

Grain from Egypt is exported all over the eastern Mediterranean.　　After fighting the Hittites, Ramesses finally makes peace with them in the twenty-first year of his reign.

Can you see who is hanging out their laundry?

Ships as far as 50 km (30 miles) away can see the lighthouse.

STUDENTS AND STREET FIGHTS

Alexandria, c. 90 BC

Founded on the orders of Alexander the Great, who conquered Egypt in 332 BC, Alexandria is a fabulously wealthy city and its Mouseion a world-famous centre of learning. Greeks, Egyptians, and Jews live here. The Greeks are a rowdy lot, rioting when anything displeases them. A king will later be killed by a rioting mob.

Temple

Lighthouse

Courtyard

Romans escaping

Students

Lictor

Greek rioters

Romans

Isis is currently Egypt's most popular goddess.

Can you see a shop owner and her dog fighting back against the rioters?

Mouseion

Harbour

Mediterranean Sea

Jetty

Theatre

Palace

School

Patient being bled

Barber

Selling medicines

Fountain house

High Priestess

King

Isis

Jewish wedding party

High Priest

Guards

Priests

Greek soldiers

31

3200 BC | 3000 | Pharaohs rule | 2500 | 2000 | 1890 | 1850 | 1500 | 1260 | 1180 | 1000 | 600 | 323 | Greeks rule | 90 | 30 | BC

Egypt becomes one kingdom   Alexander conquers Egypt | Rome conquers Egypt

GLOSSARY

Alexander the Great – (356-323 BC) King of Macedon, conqueror of an empire that reached as far as India. After he died, his generals divided his empire between them. Ptolemy became king of Egypt and his descendents ruled until 30 BC when Egypt was conquered by Rome.

Arabs – People from the Arabian Peninsula. They conquered a vast empire in the Middle East that included Egypt.

Aswan Dam – This saves the waters of the Nile's annual flood and drives turbines that produce Egypt's electricity. It was opened in 1970.

Bedouins – Nomadic desert-dwelling people who wander with their flocks. Some are also traders.

Blue Nile – River that flows from Lake Tana in the Ethiopian highlands into the White Nile near Khartoum, thus forming the Nile proper.

British – Former colonial power. It became involved in Egypt because the Suez Canal provided a quicker route to India which was part of its Empire. Britain administered Egypt as a Protectorate from 1882-1922.

Christians – Followers of Jesus Christ. Egypt was officially a Christian country from 391-640 AD.

Delta – Triangle-shaped area between Modern Cairo and the Mediterranean Sea. The Nile divides at Cairo into several channels that flow through the Delta, making it a rich farming area.

Fayum – Area of rich land southwest of modern Cairo. Its great lake was partially drained by Middle Kingdom kings to reclaim land for farming.

Habiru – An Egyptian word referring to slaves. Biblical Hebrews may have been amongst these enslaved peoples.

Karnak – The larger of the god Amun's two temples in Thebes. The smaller one is now called Luxor.

Khartoum – The capital of Sudan.

Khufu – One of the kings of Egypt. He built the largest of all the pyramids. Two of the seven boats buried in pits around his pyramid have survived. The one thought to have carried his body to the pyramid has been restored and is displayed in its own museum in Giza.

Kush – Land between the Third and Fifth Cataracts conquered by Egypt. Kush broke free of Egyptian rule in about 1000 BC and founded its own kingdom with Nubia. Around 750-663 BC Kushite kings actually ruled Egypt.

Lictor – Member of a ceremonial guard for Roman officials. Lictors carried fasces – an axe surrounded by bundles of rods – signifying their power.

Lighthouse – Tall building with a fire or light on top to guide ships to port. The lighthouse of Alexandria was one of the Seven Wonders of the World. Completed in 280 BC, earthquakes destroyed it in the 14th century AD. Stone from it was used to build a fort.

Luxor – Smaller of the god Amun's temples in Thebes.

Mamelukes – Slaves who had been trained as soldiers. They overthrew their masters, the Ayyibids, and ruled Egypt from 1250-1517 AD.

Meroe – A rich African kingdom whose culture was important from c. 600 BC-200 AD. It was finally overthrown by the King of Axum (in modern Ethiopia) c. 300 AD.

Middle Kingdom – The period from c. 2040-1650 BC. During this time the

Kings built pyramids near the Fayum. The other two great periods of Egyptian history were the Old Kingdom when the pyramids at Giza were built, and the New Kingdom when Egypt conquered a great empire.

Mouseion – Centre of scholarship in Alexandria that was created to honour the Muses (goddesses of learning).

Muezzin – Person who calls Muslims to prayers. He stands in a minaret, a tower adjoining the mosque.

Muslims – Followers of the Prophet Mohammed (c. 570-632 AD), founder of the Islamic faith.

Nubia – Land between the First and Second Cataracts, often ruled by Egypt.

Obelisk – Tall column of stone shaped at the top like a pyramid, a symbol of the sun god, Re. Pairs of obelisks were built in front of temples.

Petitioner – Person asking a god or goddess for advice. A question requiring the answer yes or no would be addressed to a statue of the god. If it became so heavy that the priests carrying it sank to the ground, or if it shook, the god was answering yes.

Pyramid – Tomb for an Egyptian king. The largest is Khufu's at Giza. It was 147 m (481 ft) tall with each side 227 m (746 ft) long. 2000 years after the pyramids at Giza were built, the Greeks named them one of the Seven Wonders of the Ancient World.

Ramesses II – King of Egypt (1290-1224 BC). He built many temples and statues as well as a new capital, Per Ramesses, in the Delta. His main enemies were the Hittites who lived in what is now Turkey. Many scholars believe he was the king the Bible mentions who enslaved the Hebrews.

Romans, Rome – Powerful nation. In the 1st century BC the Roman Empire was expanding rapidly. Rome wanted to conquer Egypt because it was wealthy and exported wheat that Rome needed to feed its people.

Saladin – Salah el Din Yusuf Ayyub (1137-1193 AD). He ruled most of the Middle East and fought Richard the Lion Heart during the Third Crusade (1182-1193 AD). His family, the Ayyibids, ruled Egypt till 1250.

Scribe – Person who reads and writes for other people in exchange for a fee.

Shrine – Place holding holy articles.

Sherden – Eastern Mediterranean people who were part of the Sea Peoples who raided Egypt. Ramesses II captured some Sherden and then hired them to fight for him.

Suez Canal – Channel linking the Mediterranean and the Red Sea. It was opened in 1869.

Thebes – Ancient city which the Egyptians called Wast, and the Greeks knew as Thebes. The modern city is called Luxor.

Turks – Muslims from Turkey. In the 16th century AD they ruled a vast empire in the Middle East. They conquered Egypt in 1517 but lost control of it under Mohammed Ali in 1811.

White Nile – River that flows from Lake Victoria through Uganda and into Sudan. At Khartoum it joins the Blue Nile to form the Nile River.

INDEX

P10-11 | P6-7   P26-27   P20-21   P8-9 | P4-5   P14-15

AD 43 | 50 | 62 | Romans rule | 300 | 640 | Arabs rule | 1190 | 1250 | 1296 | Mamelukes rule | 1517 | 1560 | Turks rule | 1840 | 1862 | 1952 | 2000

Christianity comes to Egypt   Arabs conquer Egypt   Crusades begin   Egypt becomes a Republic